Your Handbook G Backpacking Abroad

Ashley Deppeler

Preface: Having waited almost until my 21st birthday before travelling abroad my only regret is not having done so sooner. The opportunities and destinations available to travellers these days are greater than they have ever been and you can reach just about any city or town on earth within a week of departing from your home country. The idea of backpacking as an alternative way to spend a gap year or the summer holidays is becoming increasingly popular amongst younger people (18-25) as more people look to push their boundaries and experience new cultures abroad. Perhaps you've always fantasised about trekking the Inca trail in South America, or maybe your focus is to spend two weeks abroad attending your dream festival in Croatia. Whatever your plans, backpacking provides a cheap, cultural and alternative way to see the world and allows you to meet dozens of like-minded travellers along the way.

This handbook is designed to assist those of you who have planned your trip abroad but don't quite know to expect when you arrive at your destination.

Covering every aspect from arrival to departure this guide is designed to provide you with all of the essential details that I've learned over the years and provides a detailed overview of everyday travelling aspects such as accommodation and transport to those less frequent, such as bribes and haggling. While this advice is mainly aimed towards backpackers, it can also be readily used for those of you who are planning on studying or working abroad for an extended period of time or simply looking for a week away in an exotic location.

Travelling is wonderful in that it not only allows you to see historical places and sights but also allows you to step outside of your comfort zone and grow as a person. The first time you land in a foreign country can be quite intimidating, especially if the people speak a different language; however, this fear quickly subsides once you get comfortable with the idea of travelling. This is when you realise that your whole perspective of the world around you has changed and that you are capable of doing amazing things. Suddenly you don't need to speak the same language to communicate with someone, and you don't need a map to go sightseeing; it just happens. This is when you realise that you've stopped being a tourist and started becoming a traveller.

Happy travels!

Table of Contents:

Chapter 1: Arrival
Chapter 2: Accommodation
   Hostels
      Hostel Etiquette
   Hotels
   Guesthouses
   Couchsurfing
Chapter 3: Transport
   Buses and Trains
   Public Transport
   Hire Cars
   Hitchhiking
Chapter 4: Scams
   The Tuk-Tuk Salesman scam
   The 'Free' gifts scam
   The Overpriced Taxis scam
   The Flirting Woman scam
   The Closed Hotel scam
   The Helpful Local scam
   The Closed Attractions Scam
   The Rental Insurance Scam
   The Friendly Shopkeeper Scam
   Pickpockets
   Overt Theft
   Kidnapping
Chapter 5: Haggling
   Haggling
Chapter 6: Everything Else
   Day trips and walking tours

- Staying healthy
    - Food Poisoning
    - Bed Bugs
    - Rabies and Tetanus
    - Sunburn
- Being considerate
- Tipping and Donations
- Insurance Claims
- Contacting Home
    - Calling home
    - Mail
- Departure Tax and bribes

Chapter 1: Arrival

On arrival to your destination, be sure to have your passport, accommodation details, arrival card, visa if necessary, proof of funds documents and cash ready for any on arrival visa fees you may need to pay and any other questions you may encounter. If you've crossed into the country via a land border, any questions will likely occur at the border, while those arriving by plane will be shuttled through immigration at the airport. It's important to fill out your arrival card correctly and fill in as much information as correctly as possible as failure to fill in your initial address may result in several hours of questioning, while failure to produce a departure ticket may lead some immigration officers to assume you're seeking to stay in the country longer than you're claiming to seek work instead. If you're given documents by immigration hold on to them, as they may be required again upon leaving the country.

When you've arrived at your hostel and checked in grab one of their business cards from the front counter and put it in your wallet, it's worth its weight in gold if you get lost or need to get directions. While the temptation on arrival may be to go out straight away and start sightseeing, it's often better to take a shower, change your clothes and begin adjusting to the local time zone by eating the closest meal to match the current time of day. If you've arrived in the early hours of the morning it's often best to try and get at least 3-4 hours of sleep before morning while arriving in the afternoon is generally the best time as this gives you several hours to soak up the new atmosphere before retiring to catch up on some much-needed rest. If you arrive in the evening it's best to have a light meal and then get your body clock in sync by sleeping, you can always set your alarm for an early start the following morning and head out then.

Once you've showered, slept and eaten, it's a good idea to locate the nearest supermarket to go and buy your groceries from. For most travellers quantity takes preference over quality when purchasing food so look for things such as pasta, bread, soups, cereals and noodles to make up the bulk of your meals while you can add things such as meat, cheese and vegetables to taste while milk is great for cereal, tea and coffee if the hostel doesn't already provide some. Be sure to buy fruit or nuts as well to cover your allotment of cheap and easy snacks throughout the day. Not only does this help tick off your health quota for the day it will also save you quite a large amount of money over the duration of your trip, as eating out or getting street food every day can quickly add up. For those of you who would rather avoid vast quantities of carbs look to buy items that are equally as cheap yet much healthier such as brown rice, lentils, vegetables and spices to provide some extra flavour and variety in your meals. It's worth asking around or searching online for cheap and easy vegetarian meals as these will keep you feeling full and healthier than eating spaghetti bolognese every day will.

When you're ready to get out and start exploring your new surroundings take the opportunity to do so as a local rather than a tourist and keep the map in your pocket while you go for your first walk around the city. By now you've likely seen how the locals dress and try and it's best to try and match their fashions rather than imposing your own, as this will only highlight you as a tourist and you're more likely to draw unwanted attention to yourself in the process. Unless you've arrived in a city with a high rate of crime you should be free from too much harassment during the day time and most areas should be safe to walk so take the time to explore back alleys, side streets and non-touristic areas during this time as it allows you to see a richer and more authentic side of your location. When it's time to turn around and head back to the hostel you can do so by consulting your map or by asking directions, using the hostel's business card you collected on arrival as your address.

Chapter 2: Accommodation

Hostels

Depending on your travelling style you've either booked your accommodation prior to arriving in a new location or you're happy to turn up in a new place and find a hostel once you arrive. While both of these styles have their pros and cons, it's beneficial to check websites such as Tripadvisor.com, Hostelworld.com or Hostelbookers.com for reviews prior to booking or checking into a hostel. When checking accommodation reviews, be sure to take into account reviews that mention the following:

- Bedbugs - Even the cleanest and best hostels can find themselves with a sudden burst of bedbug related incidents if these nasty little vermin get brought in from elsewhere via rucksacks and bedding. If the hostel has recent reviews that mention bedbugs, or they seem to have an ongoing problem with them, then it's best to avoid the place altogether if you're looking for a good night's sleep.

- Theft - Some hostels have higher instances of theft, either due to their poor layout or facilities or the fact the staff themselves have light fingers. As with bedbugs make note of recent reviews that mention theft, or reviews where guests mention having stuff taken from their locker.

- Location - Even the best hostel in the world can antagonise a weary traveller if it's located in the middle of nowhere or in an area that should be avoided. Always check to see where the hostel is located relative to the city centre and other accommodation, as hostels located near major attractions and other hostels tend to be easier to find and better well known. Additionally if you arrive and find that they are full, then you're able to seek accommodation somewhere close by, rather than being stranded on the wrong side of the city to everything else.

While the above are three key things that will assist you in finding a decent hostel be sure to take the time to review the one star reviews of potential hostels, as these outline the worst experiences travellers have had there as well as the overall ranking of the hostel relative to other hostels. Take into account the check-in times, facilities such as lockers and Wi-Fi as well as extras such as breakfast and social activities when making a booking, as sometimes paying a slightly higher price for a hostel can actually save you money if they include breakfast, dinner or a tour in the price of your stay. Likewise, reviews will give you a good overview of what kind of hostel it is, some hostels play up the party angle and as such you're unlikely to get a lot of sleep while others may have an 11:00pm lights out policy and are perfect for a couple of days spent recuperating during your trip.

When checking the price for a hostel use Tripadvisor.com for comparison prices, as they are not a booking agent as such and show the booking prices for several websites rather than just one. Also take a few moments to check if the hostel itself has a website which you can book through as it may be that they are able to offer cheaper prices through their own site than through affiliate sites such as

Hostelworld and Hostel Booker. Additionally in the event that a hostel is accidently overbooked staff are more likely to give preference to people who have booked through the hostel site directly rather than through a third party.

Hostel Etiquette

While each hostel has their own etiquette and expectations from guests, there are a few general rules you should adhere to when staying at a hostel to avoid antagonising staff and other guests:

- Don't turn the light on when entering a room - Nothing is more likely to put you offside with your roommates than arriving back at the hostel at night, walking into the room and then turning on the light while you rummage around in your rucksack looking for your pyjamas or your phone charger. When entering your room during the evening be considerate of the fact that other people may be sleeping and use the light from your phone to illuminate your way when getting into bed or searching for something. This also goes for loud things such as zips and plastic bags, which can also wake other travellers. If you must turn on a light or make a noise try to be as respectful as possible and keep it to a minimum.

- Know your fridge etiquette - Unless it's explicitly marked as 'free' or 'communal' don't help yourself to food that's been sitting in the fridge as it likely belongs to another traveller. Hostel fridges often get cleaned out weekly by staff to get rid of old or unwanted food so ensure that you put your name on anything that you're storing in the fridge. Additionally if you're extra cautious, you can also put your check out date on the items as well, as staff will then know not to throw this out when the fridge is next cleaned.

- Clean up after yourself - It goes without saying that you should clean up after yourself when staying in a hostel, yet it's something that seems to fall by the wayside a lot of the time for some travellers. If you use plates, cups, cutlery, etc., be sure to clean them and put them away after use. Likewise, try not to let your stuff take up too much space in your room, as it's likely to intrude on other people's space.

- Keep your hookups low key - If you happen to meet someone or someones during the course of your trip then try and avoid having sex in a location that's going to subject other people to a running audio commentary of everything that's going on.

- Be social - Even if you're the most anti-social introvert in the world you can still say 'hello' to people, especially if you're sharing a room with them. Travelling is a great time to meet people as you already have something in common and a lot to talk about with the people that you meet such as travel plans, attractions and stories.

Hotels

While hotels almost always more expensive than hostels you may find that in some places hostels do not exist or you're simply happy to spend a bit extra to spend the night in a place with a decent hot water supply and a decent double bed (though this isn't always the case). Likewise after a long haul flight a hotel can be a great starting point to acclimatise yourself with your new surrounds for the first 24 hours as you don't have to worry about check-in times or other guests and can often arrange an airport transfer if you're a little apprehensive about catching a bus or taxi into the city. As with hostels, Trip Advisor is your best bet for finding the best price for a hotel, although lastminute.com can also offer some decent bargains, as well as can booking directly through the hotel site. Always compare prices between the three sites as somewhat surprisingly it may be cheaper to book through a third party rather than directly through the hotels website.

Guesthouses

Commonly referred to a 'Bed and Breakfast' finding a good guesthouse can sometimes be an art form; however, the decision can be well worth it if you find a nice place to stay. Often found in places such as the Balkans and Africa guesthouses offer guests the opportunity to see life through that of a local, as you're normally staying in an offshoot of their own home. While the price and quality of guesthouses can fluctuate greatly depending on the time of year and demand it's well worth considering a guest house as an alternative to hostels or hotels when you're looking for something quiet and informal. While guesthouses can be difficult to locate online, largely owing to the fact that a lot of guesthouse operators don't speak English, in a lot of instances you will be met directly off the bus by several people all offering you accommodation at their house and you can find yourself spoilt for choice. If you're worried about ending up in a poor quality guest house, you can always insist on first checking it out before committing to staying and handing over money.

Couchsurfing

Chances are if you're not staying in a hostel, hotel or at a private residence then you're trying your hand at Couchsurfing instead. Since its foundation in 2004 Couchsurfing has become one of the biggest alternative means of finding accommodation in the world and features over 9 million members worldwide. If you've found a host, there are a few things you can do to ensure that your experience is as enjoyable as possible for both you and your host:

- Keep your host informed - While not always possible endeavour to keep your host as informed as possible about your expected arrival and departure times so they can adjust their schedule accordingly. If you're running late endeavour to let them know your new expected arrival time via a text message or a message on Couchsurfing.

- Bring a small gift to say thank you on arrival - While some people may prefer to give a small gift at the end of their stay it's often better received to do so at the start, as this shows that you're thankful for their offer to host you before you've spent time with your host. It can also go a long way to building rapport with your host and gives a great chance to talk about the gift and why you've chosen it.

- Ask before helping yourself - While most hosts will say to make yourself at home once you've arrived, it's always polite to ask before helping yourself to their tea and coffee or throwing a load of laundry in the washing machine.

- Let the host set their level of involvement - Some hosts will spend most of your stay at work or university and may only join you for a night out while others will take the time to show you around the city and give you a guided tour of sorts as well as taking you out of an evening. Depending on the host and their current schedule this will vary so while it's great to ask a host about what you should see and do while visiting their city, you should never expect or ask them to take you to see these attractions, as they will offer if they're prepared to do so.

- Offer to cook - Even if you're the worst cook in the world Couchsurfing is a great chance to share some of your local cuisine with your host. If you're not able to cook anything from your home country, then even something simple like pasta will be appreciated and can be done quite cheap. Take the chance to check out a market for fresh produce and ingredients and experience grocery shopping from a local perspective. Likewise, once a meal is finished, it's always great to do the washing up. It only takes a few minutes and it's much appreciated by the host.

- Don't bring back other guests or friends - Unless you've got explicit permission from a host before doing so it is never good to bring someone else back to your host's house as this is likely to be considered rude or inappropriate.

- Leave a review - Upon departure take a few moments to leave a review for the host and mention the highlights of the stay as well as reasons why other Couchsurfers should stay with your host.

Chapter 3: Transport

Buses and Trains

Travelling by bus or train is by far the most popular method of transport for backpackers, as it's often cheap, scenic and provides a chance to get some sleep in between destinations. While it's possible to book busses and trains in the months leading up to your trip, there's a large majority of travellers who prefer to book in the 48 hours leading up to departure for the added flexibility when travelling. Nonetheless, no matter what your travelling style is there are a few things you can do to ensure that your journey goes as smoothly as possible:

- Book in advance where possible - Busses and trains on popular tourist routes can prove popular and sell out days or even weeks in advance, so it's in your best interests to book early when you can. Additionally, booking in advance can be cheaper, especially in places such as Ireland or France where prices get more expensive as the departure date gets closer. If you're looking for more flexibility in travelling then be prepared to pay this higher price to do so. Likewise, if you're looking to travel as cheaply as possible and don't like the idea of hitchhiking then you'll need to trade some flexibility for a cheaper price and book in advance.

- Take a small day bag onboard - If you're stowing your luggage underneath the bus or in the overhead racks on a train then consider taking a day bag with you onboard, containing things you may need during the trip such as your passport, cash, water, snacks, phone, chargers, deodorant, Kindle, book or laptop or tablet if you have one.

- Go to the toilet before boarding - Unless you're certain your bus has toilet facilities on board or it's only a short distance between destinations a quick toilet stop before boarding can save you a lot of troubles during the trip. Likewise, if there are no toilet facilities onboard avoid drinking copious amounts of water as it could be a long time between rest stops.

- Sit in your correct seat - While it's often a mad scramble for train and bus seating, take the time to locate your correct seat (or bed) when boarding the train or bus as this can save you a lot of hassle later on if you're asked to move by the correct owner of the seat you're currently in. If unsure, ask a conductor or the driver and they will be happy to point you in the right direction.

- Take a chance to stretch - If you're on an extended bus or train trip take the opportunity to get up occasionally and go for a walk at a rest stop or up and down the aisle. Not only will this keep you awake, it will also give you a chance to get away from the stuffy cramped conditions of your cabin or seat.

Public Transport

Public transport is often the cheapest and most convenient way to get around a city or town, though the price and availability may vary depending on your location. Ensure that you buy a ticket before using the public transport as failure to do so can sometime result in an exorbitant fine which either needs to be paid immediately or at a later date. Where possible use public transport to and from the airport, making a note of the first and last trip times for your arrival and departure day to ensure you're not left stranded in the city when you have a 5am arrival or flight. Likewise, note the price of airport trips as most places charge extra for airport transfers on top of the usual ticket price. Ensure that you buy a ticket before boarding the train or bus as it's common to see ticket inspectors taking advantage of newly arrived tourists by checking tickets on the airport transfer services.

Take the time to find out if there are special tourist passes available at a cheaper price or if it's easier to buy an everyday pass instead. Find the right ticket to match your intended length of stay (24 hours, 48 hours, weekly, etc.) and make a note of what constitutes acceptable proof if you're purchasing a concession card, as a student card from a foreign country or an International Student Card is not a valid concession. When in doubt buy the more expensive option, as you're still liable to pay a fine if you're carrying the wrong kind of ticket. Most cities have free maps available which outline bus, train and tram stops and these can usually be collected for free from airport information booths, tourist information booths or from your hostel.

Hire Cars

If you're travelling frequently and for a set period of time (e.g., two weeks) it's well worth looking into hiring a car, especially in places such as Europe and Australia where public transport can be quite expensive. Quotes can often be obtained online and most car rental operators have dozens of drop off points when returning your vehicle, meaning you're unlikely to have to double back to drop off your car at the end of the trip. Hire cars offer additional flexibility in your travel schedule and allow you to visit more places than you might otherwise be able to see by taking public transport. The downside of hire cars is that you run the risk of getting lost, even with the GPS and you are responsible for the car while you're renting it, meaning that you're not able to disappear off on tours for days at a time.

Hitchhiking

By far the cheapest and most adventurous way to travel is by hitchhiking. While this method isn't for everyone, especially those on a tight schedule, it can be a very fun and rewarding experience when travelling. If you're considering hitchhiking take the time to review the legalities of doing so in your destinations and see what your chances are of scoring a lift, as some places are much more open to the practice than others. For first time hitchhikers, there are several important things you can do to ensure that you find a ride and stay safe during your travels:

- Use a map - Given the sometimes stop-start nature of hitchhiking, a good map is an invaluable tool to have, especially if it highlights things such as rest stops or petrol stations. A map with an at least 1:1,000,000 ratio will suffice if needed while 1:750,000 should normally be good enough. If your phone or tablet is capable of doing so it may also help to map your intended route into the phone, which can also assist you in determining your location should you get lost or disoriented.

- Find a good, safe location - If you're looking to hitch it may be tempting to walk to a major street or highway and simply try from there; however, this could prove to be more time-consuming than useful. Find a major highway or road that leads towards your destination to reduce the amount of local traffic and position yourself on the side of the road where you are clearly visible to oncoming traffic and they have enough space to stop and pick you up.

- Have a sign outlining your destination - Having a clearly visible sign greatly improves your chances of getting a lift and getting to your intended destination, even if your intended destination is as vague as 'South' or 'France'. Additionally you can add a few words of the local language in 'Por Favor' for instance, or use abbreviations for cities rather than full names, such a 'KRK' for Krakow or 'HH' for Hamburg.

- Dress appropriately - You're much more likely to get a lift if you're dressed like a trustworthy and honest person. Resist the urge to wear sunglasses or a hoodie when trying to thumb a lift and wear neutral or pale colours if possible, as these appear more trustworthy than black or khaki clothing.

- Trust your instincts - If someone stops and offers you a ride, but you're getting a bad vibe from them, it's best to decline, even if they're the only person who's stopped for some time. It's better to wait a while longer for a ride than to go against your instincts and get in a vehicle with someone who you're not entirely comfortable with.

- Note the details of the vehicle - As an added safety precaution note the details of the vehicle before you get in, including the brand, model, colour and license plate number of the car. Write these down or put them in your phone and, if possible, message them to a friend. If asked explain that this is a precautionary measure and most drivers will understand this. You can also make a joke that your Mum insists you text her the details every time you hitch a lift as she worries about you far too much.

Chapter 4: Scams

It's inevitable that at some point while traveling abroad you will be approached by somebody looking to fleece you of your money or valuables. Their method may be subtle, such as inflating otherwise reasonable prices or it could be overtly obvious, such as demanding cash or falling victim to a snatch and grab theft. While being scammed may sound like an intimidating thought this shouldn't deter you from getting out and seeing things while travelling, indeed being scammed is something that's happened to every traveller at some stage. If you happen upon a traveller who claims that they've never been scammed then they're either lying or they're incredibly gullible and simply haven't realised. To give you an advantage in scam detection here's twelve of the most common scam techniques that you're likely to encounter.

The Tuk-Tuk Salesman scam

Common in: India, Thailand.

Perhaps one of the most prevalent scams in Asia; a dodgy tuk-tuk driver will offer to take you to carpet or gem stores where you will proceed to be offered deals so good it would be stupid to pass them up. Far from good deals, these carpets, gems, artefacts or works of art are often worthless replicas or low-quality merchandise which you've just paid far too much for. To make things worse, the tuk-tuk driver often returns later on to receive his cut of the sale, a commission that ensures he will continue bringing gullible tourists to the same stores in the future.

How to avoid this scam:
Firstly don't allow yourself to be taken on an impromptu shopping excursion with your new found friend, as they aren't looking to assist you in getting a good deal. If you're looking at buying souvenirs while abroad, take the time to research what to look for when detecting a low quality or fake item and be prepared to walk away from a sale, as a reputable salesman will understand you taking the time to research before returning. If in doubt,

either avoid purchasing the item altogether or buy it at a price you'd feel comfortable paying if you later found out it's fake.

The 'Free' gifts scam
Common in: Europe
Wandering around near a major tourist attraction you're approached by someone carrying a collection of flowers, cd's or bracelets and they will give you one, stating that it's a gift as they tie the bracelet around your wrist, sign the cd or hand you the flower. As you thank them and begin to leave, they will then demand money for the 'gift' and can get abusive until you cough up a price for the purchase. These scams often rely on intimidation or guilt tripping you into making the purchase, as most people will often cough up the asking price to get away from the situation.

How to avoid this scam:
Firstly be wary of anyone approaching you with a large collection of anything, be it flowers, cd's, maps, etc. They're not standing around all day giving out items for free out of the goodness of their

heart and they will eventually demand money from you. Simply keep walking and ignore them completely. If they've handed you the item, simply place it on the ground and walk away or if you're unable to do so as it's a bracelet tied to your wrist then just walk away. You may receive some abuse for doing so; however, they will eventually give up and go back to looking for new victims.

The Overpriced Taxis scam
Common in: Europe, Asia, Las Vegas
A scam that can be hard to recognise if you're unfamiliar with a city the overpriced taxi scam can occur in three forms, dodgy meters, dodgy routes or dodgy deals. The first occurs when a driver either installs a fake taxi meter that charges a much higher price than it normally should or they use the wrong rate to artificially bump up the price such as an off peak night rate instead of the correct peak daytime rate. The second involves the driver taking a much longer route than required to get to your destination, thereby bumping up the price of an otherwise cheaper trip while the third will see a driver demand

more than the original price that you've bargained for or ask you to cough up for the toll booths along the way.

How to avoid this scam:
If possible get an idea of the approximate price for your trip before you go searching for a taxi. Airports often have a fixed rate for trips to and from the city and these can often be found by asking at information booths or taxi stands in the airport. If you're unsure as to how much a trip should be, consider asking a local or bartering with a driver on the price, settling on something you think is reasonable. Be prepared to skip a driver who demands an exorbitant fee, as there is always someone who will take you for a lower fare. When possible, keep your luggage within reach rather than in the boot of the taxi, as it gives you a better bargaining position if the taxi driver cannot keep your rucksack hostage. When possible, always agree on a price before getting into the vehicle and double check the price, to ensure that they cannot claim a miscommunication. If asked to pay an

additional fare for toll booths, politely refuse, citing that this is included in the price of a taxi fare.

The Flirting Woman scam

Common in: Poland, Thailand, Vietnam

Out one evening taking in the cities nightlife, you're approached by a gorgeous and friendly woman who explains that she's just arrived in the city or is looking for somewhere to go out for a drink. Taking an interest in you she suggests a nearby bar and you go together for a drink, whereby you're presented for an extortionately large bill for the drinks and discover that should you try and leave, there are several very intimidating looking men who will prevent you from doing so until the bill is paid. Particularly potent versions of this scam can also see your drink spiked, resulting in a much nastier experience and potentially a hospital visit as well.

How to avoid this scam:
If you're approached by anybody on the street who asks you to go for a drink the best approach is to accept their offer, insist on your choice of bar rather than going to one they've suggested. If they're

genuinely interested in having a drink with you then they will accept this offer, whereas those women simply looking to scam you will quickly lose interest in the idea once you've insisted on going elsewhere. If you find yourself in the bar and are confronted for payment always put your safety first and pay rather than trying to argue your way out of the situation. If possible, bargain the scammers down on price as some will ask for an exorbitant figure and then, with some haggling, accept a lower price as it makes you more likely to pay and they can then move on to their next victim.

The Closed Hotel scam

Common in: Europe, Asia

Arriving in a new country you step out of the airport or bus station, find a taxi and show the driver the address of your hostel. As you head towards your destination, he checks the address again, suddenly realising that your hostel is actually closed or has recently burnt down, but he knows of a hotel nearby that you can stay in instead. In reality, your hostel is still open and the driver is simply trying to take you to a hotel instead because he gets a commission from the hotel for people that opt to stay in the hotel.

How to avoid this scam:
Insist on being taken to the address of your hostel rather than letting the driver dictate the course. If needed call the hostel to confirm that they are indeed open or state that you called them upon arriving and yes, they are open. Most drivers won't push the subject too far, especially when presented with evidence that the hostel is indeed open. In the event the driver arrives at the wrong location anyway, be prepared to walk away and find a new driver if there is one nearby or threaten to call the police.

The Helpful Local scam

Common in: India, Cambodia, Morocco
Wandering around the city centre you find yourself consulting a map while trying to figure out where you are or which direction you should be going in. A friendly local approaches you and offers directions or to take you to your intended

destination. Thankful you accept their offer and upon providing directions or arriving at your destination they will demand a fee for doing so, often trying to block you from leaving until it's paid.

How to avoid this scam:
This scam can be difficult to detect until after it's happened as most of the time friendly locals will genuinely offer to assist you in finding your way around. Use your judgement in situations where people offer to take you there, instead preferring directions if you're unsure. In the event that someone makes a point of approaching you as soon as you've pulled out your map or phone then they're likely more likely to be a scammer. If lost seek out a local rather than waiting on someone to approach you or better yet, go to a nearby store or hotel and ask for directions as the person behind the counter does not have an ulterior motive in helping you.

The Closed Attractions Scam
Common in: India, Thailand, Cambodia

You climb into a tuk-tuk or taxi and ask to be taken to a particular tourist attraction and the driver is happy to oblige. Along the way he 'remembers' that the attraction is actually closed today because it's The King's Birthday/Monday/Under Reconstruction; however, he does know of a different attraction nearby which is open and he's happy to take you there instead. Upon doing so, you're expected to pay to enter this attraction and the driver receives a commission for bringing you along.

How to avoid this scam:
When possible ask at the hostel before leaving to visit the attraction to establish when the attractions opening hours are or insist on being taken there anyway as you 'want to take some photos around the area' instead. If you're taken to an alternative attraction, be prepared to exit the tuk-tuk or taxi to find a new driver or politely insist that you're not interested in this attraction at all and that you'd rather go somewhere else instead.

The Rental Insurance Scam

Common in: Thailand, Indonesia

You arrive at your location and discover that you can hire a scooter/car/jet ski/motorbike for a reasonable price. You pay the rental price, leave a deposit or credit card details as insurance, and upon returning the item, the renter points out the 'damage' that you've caused and demands an exorbitant sum of money to pay for these damages. In some instances the renter may even threaten to call the police if you don't pay up, and attempting to call this bluff can often backfire as the police can side with the local and demand their own 'fine' on top not to press charges for the damage.

How to avoid this scam:
If you would like to hire a car/scooter/motorbike/jet ski take the time to inspect it before doing so and document all of the current superficial damages with the renter present. Avoid handing over ID instead of cash as a deposit, as it's much easier to bargain down or walk away when the renter isn't

implicitly holding your passport hostage. Where possible rent from somewhere recommended by your hostel, they may make a small cut in some cases but it's better to go with a reputable rental agency and pay a little higher fee for doing so than find yourself in a precarious position paying much more to a scammer.

The Friendly Shopkeeper Scam

Common in: Turkey, India, Sri Lanka, Morocco
Wandering around the city you are approached by a friendly local who compliments you on something or asks you how you're finding their country. After some small talk, they invite you to their shop, promising to show you how they ply their trade or offering bargains that you won't find elsewhere. Upon going in, you're often presented with tea and are subjected to a sales pitch and pushy sales tactics to try and get you to purchase goods from their store.

How to avoid this scam:
Be cautious of people approaching you on the street and offering to take you somewhere nearby.

Likewise, avoid being drawn into a conversation or promising to take a quick look, as it's easier to walk away now than it is to do so later once you're inside the store. If they persist, explain that you're on a tight schedule and simply don't have the time right now.

Pickpockets

Common in: Spain, France, Italy, Czech Republic, Argentina

Perhaps the most well-known scam pickpocketing often occurs on public transport or in crowded areas where pickpockets are able to get close to a victim without arousing suspicion. Pickpockets are often ingenious in their methods and this can range from having an accomplice throw something on you which the pickpocket then generously offers to wipe off for you or stops to offer you directions as an accomplice goes through your pockets while you are distracted. Additionally gangs of pickpockets often target public transport, especially airport trains, where they can go unnoticed as they press up against people and lightly rob them of their valuables. This can also extend to pickpockets using a knife to cut open a hole in your bag to access your stuff inside or even having an accomplice approach you warning you to check your stuff as they've heard there are pickpockets in the area. By checking your stuff, you're giving the pickpocket a green light as to the location of your valuables and making yourself a target.

How to avoid this scam:
Firstly keep your valuables in a secure location when travelling, meaning that your phone and wallet should be kept in your internal pockets in your jacket where possible and not in a location where it's visible and easy to access. Ultimately pickpockets are going to go after people who look like easy targets and they are often so skilled you won't even realise until after you've been pickpocketed, so it's important to be aware of your surrounds, especially if someone approaches you or is acting unusually. If you're concerned that you may have been pickpocketed, move off the street to a nearby store or hotel before checking your

valuables and avoid taking anything with you that you're not prepared to lose.

Overt Theft

Common in: Greece, Romania, Thailand
While pickpockets may be discreet, there are people who choose to be more obvious when attempting to steal your valuables and may simply do so in a snatch and grab attack or by driving off with your valuables still in the vehicle. These types of incidents are often opportunistic rather than elaborately planned and often occur in busy tourist areas such as outside attractions or outdoor cafes.

How to avoid this scam:
Keep items such as your camera and other valuables on you at all times rather than sitting on a bench or table. If you are seated somewhere and would like to put your valuables down put them as close as possible and on the opposite side to the nearest exit, as it makes it harder to a potential thief to snatch the item from the table. If you need to leave your stuff unattended ask the staff if you can store it somewhere for a moment. If they're unable to do so

ask them and another patron to keep an eye on it while you're gone and take anything of value, including your passport, cash and phone.

Kidnapping

Common in: Mexico, Venezuela, Lebanon, Brazil
You find yourself approached by a man or a group of men who offer to assist you or show you around. When you refuse they begin to threaten or intimidate you and force you into a car, whereby you're informed that you'll be kept hostage until you meet their demands for payment. If you're not able to pay the kidnappers may contact your family or friends instead seeking a ransom to release you, though this is much less common than 'express' kidnappings where the hostage meets the demands themselves.

How to avoid this scam:
Travel in daylight hours and avoid visiting towns and cities prone to kidnapping. Take care to research up to date information, particularly if travelling to South America. If you are kidnapped,

comply with your kidnapper's demands and ensure that you avoid antagonising them where possible. More often than not kidnappers are simply looking for the ransom and are not interested in hurting you; however, if you're unable to produce the cash or irritate them more than other kidnapping victims this situation can turn more sinister than it already is.

The best thing you can do if you see that someone is trying to scam you is to be polite but firm in refusing their advances or proposals, as yelling at or abusing the scammer is only going to escalate an otherwise calm situation into one much more serious. Likewise if you realise you've been scammed, especially for smaller scams, it's often better to walk away and chalk it up to experience than to confront the scammer and demand your money back, unless you're confident that doing so will not put you in a potentially dangerous position.

Chapter 5: Haggling

Haggling

To most western people, the idea of haggling is both fun and intimidating, especially for first timers. Seldom do we get the chance to test our haggling skills at a market or store and it can be quite a shock to suddenly find yourself in an environment where you're expected to haggle for almost everything, from taxis to food to accommodation. Ultimately the purpose of haggling is to arrive at a price that you feel comfortable paying and the vendor feels comfortable selling at. While haggling can seem like a daunting prospect there are several things you can do to ensure you get the best deal:

- Be polite throughout the bargaining - Haggling is one of the oldest concepts known to man and is deeply rooted in the values of numerous cultures. By engaging in the process of haggling it's expected that you will adhere to these values and maintain a polite and civil tone throughout the process.

- Let the salesman give you the opening price - Giving the opening price as a potential buyer is a great way of exposing yourself as an amateur haggler and leaves you with very little manoeuvrability when it comes to setting a price, as your initial offer may be far higher than anything the vendor expects to earn for the goods and the only way is upwards in price.

- Make your opening offer low but not insulting - This can be difficult to gauge depending on your location as every culture has their own expectations on what constitutes a reasonable opening offer. A good rule of thumb is to start at 25% of the asking price and then work your way upwards from there; however, some locations, such as China, you can start the bargaining process with as little as one percent of the asking price on some goods such as electronics or fake clothing.

- Bargain in progressively smaller increments - Ensure that your bargaining has a pattern that suggests you're nearing your maximum. There's no point opening with 1200 rupees before going 1250, 1400, 1425, 1500, 1600 as this will suggest you're more open to paying a higher price, while 1200, 1350, 1450, 1500, 1525, 1540 shows that you're getting close to a price point you're happy with.

- Mention that you can get it cheaper elsewhere - If you're in a busy marketplace, it's highly likely there are two, three or even a dozen different stalls all selling the same goods that you are currently looking to purchase. A useful technique for lowering the price is to mention that you can get the same item for a lower price elsewhere.

- Add more to the deal - If you're looking to purchase two shirts it's always good to start the bargaining with a negotiation over one shirt rather than both, as this gives you greater leverage later on as it's always better for the salesman to sell two shirts rather than one. If you've negotiated a price of 150 rupees for one shirt start the process again for adding a second shirt, how about two for 280 instead?

- Don't insult the person or the goods - Haggling is a fun activity and one that warrants respect from both parties. Don't insult the salesman or the quality of the goods during the bargaining process as this will only make the negotiations less friendly rather than getting you a better deal. If you feel the need to critique the quality mention that the shirt is slightly too big or slightly too small to fit you properly rather than pointing out the stitching is inferior or the quality is poor.

- Be prepared to walk away - Perhaps the most underutilised tool in your haggling arsenal is being prepared to walk away if you're unable to reach a price you want. Often this will determine if the salesman was correct when he said that he was unable to go any lower on price, as a sale for a lower price is better than no sale at all and he's about to lose that sale. If he's unwilling or unable to lower the price even after you've left then you know that is the lowest he's prepared to go on the price and you can always return later to buy it.

So what should a typical haggling conversation look like? To use an example from a market stall purchasing two shirts the conversation should normally go as follows if you're browsing shirts at a particular stall:

Shopkeeper: Hello my friend, perhaps you want to buy some shirts today?

You: Yeah, I'm interested in buying one if I can find something I like, how much do you have on this one?

S: This shirt is good quality and for you I can do a very good price, 250 rupees.

Y: Hmm 220 rupees is quite high for a shirt like this, I can do you 80 rupees for it though.

S: 80 rupees? No, my friend, this shirt is very good quality, see it's 'Armani', very good brand. I can sell for 220 rupees only.

Y: Hmm yes it is quite a nice shirt but 200 is still too much, I can buy it for 200 from the other store. I'll give you 120 rupees for it.

S: 120 for this? No, my friend, I cannot sell so low, this is worth at least 180.

Y: 180 rupees? I can do 135, this shirt might not even fit me yet.
S: It will fit, is perfect size for you. 160 rupees, special price.
Y: Ok I'll give you 145 if I can buy two shirts for this price. 290 total.
S: Ok my friend, for you, both shirts for 300.
Y: Deal.

While this whole exchange can take anywhere from 15 seconds through to several minutes as each side dramatises their offers the above is an example of finding the right price for goods purchased from a market. Even goods with a fixed price attached to them can be negotiated, though the overall markdown may be lower than in the example above. Keep in mind that if your friends have purchased an item from the same store previously, it's quite rude to walk up and demand the same price as your friend got, it's normally expected that you will engage in the same bartering process your friend did in order to get the same deal.

Chapter 6: Everything Else

Day trips and walking tours

Often run by accommodation providers and private companies, day trips and tours give you the chance to see and learn about sights that you might otherwise not had the opportunity to see. The price of day trips can fluctuate wildly depending on the size of the group, the duration of the trip, the trip provider, the time of year and the language spoken by the guide so it pays to shop around and check online to see what trips are available.

In some instances paying for a day trip is preferable to trying to visit the locations yourself due to public transport constraints, distance or time taken and many reputable companies will offer an enjoyable experience for travellers rather than leaving you feeling like you've been dragged from one location to another. Be sure to ask the staff at your hostel for any recommendations, but do note that while some will go ahead and book your chosen tour for you others may subtly try and sell you on a tour which earns them a commission on referrals. Before booking a day trip make note of the leaving destination and time to ensure you're not waking up an hour earlier than you would like to and having to trek to the departure point.

Walking tours are an immensely popular and varied way of seeing a city, often encompassing a wide variety of historical topics and locations. While the price for walking tours may vary dependant on the operator, subject or duration most cities will have several free walking tours available which are a great way to see the city without paying too much, as these operators work on a 'pay as you feel' basis rather than a set price. Much like day trips tours operate at different times of the day dependant on season so it's worth asking at your hostel or checking online to see when and where these tours depart from.

Staying healthy

While travelling can be an enjoyable and interesting experience it can also be incredibly tiring at times and you may notice a decline in your overall feeling of wellbeing as well, particularly if you are adjusting to an entirely new diet, eating food that's prepared less sanitarily than you would normally eat or you're taking preventative medications such as malaria tablets. With that being said there are several things you can do to keep your health in good shape and your energy levels up:

- Rest - While the temptation is always there to spend every night drinking, and it's hard not to do so when staying in a hostel, you'll feel a lot better overall if you get at least one solid 8 hour night of sleep at least twice a week. This will keep you feeling fresh and energetic for the nights you do go out and you'll find yourself enjoying those nights a lot more.

- Diet - Admittedly your diet will suffer while you're travelling, as cooked meals give way to take away and quantity takes preference over quality when it comes to purchasing food. If possible take a multivitamin, try and eat as much fruit and vegetables as you can and drink plenty of water. While you're not looking to embark on a diet while travelling you do want to at least make an effort to eat healthy some of the time.

- Alcohol - Much like diet it's quite unreasonable to expect that you'll only go out 1-2 nights per week when travelling; however, like your diet, it's important to try and include the odd alcohol free day in there when you can. The temptation will be there almost every night to go out and drink, nevertheless 1-2 alcohol free nights per week will give your body a bit of time to catch up with your newfound regime of partying and you'll notice the difference on those couple of hangover free days.
- Days off - While it may sound absurd to take a day off from holidays it's important for people travelling for longer periods of time to take the occasional day where they do as little as possible and just relax, if you're not already. Sure, it might be fun to do day trips seven days a week; however, you'll find that you can maintain an intense sightseeing regime for a much longer period of time if you take the

occasional day off. It's also a great chance to get some washing done, catch up on emails, upload some photos and binge watch any television series you may have fallen behind in.

Food Poisoning

Chances are if you're travelling you will at some stage encounter a bout of food poisoning, despite your best precautions. While you may have a higher likelihood while travelling there are preventative actions you can take to minimise the risk of food poisoning:

- Wash your hands before eating - Washing your hands before eating can reduce the risk of contracting food poisoning. In areas where you're unlikely to find soap or clean water try using antiseptic wipes instead as these will also do a good job of removing germs and bacteria.

- Avoid drinks that contain tap water - If you're in an area where the quality of the tap water is questionable then stick to bottled water during your trip. This also applies to ice cubes in drinks, as ice is often prepared with local tap water rather than bottled or spring water.

- Avoid reheated food - Where possible avoid reheated food such as those found at buffets and in bain-maries. If it looks like it's been sitting there for a while, it may be unsafe to eat and should be avoided.

- Avoid certain foods - The adage that you should avoid anything that hasn't been 'boiled, peeled or cooked' is well documented and this extends to food such as fresh salads, melons and meats which may have been left out for a prolonged period of time.

- Eat food from clean places - Street food can be cheap and delicious if prepared properly; however, if the stall operator is showing little regard for hygiene and there're flies settling on the food then it may be best to look elsewhere. Likewise, if you go into a restaurant and notice that there are cats, dogs, mice or rats wandering around in front of house, it's highly likely that the same thing is happening back of house, as well where your food is being prepared for service.

While symptoms can vary in intensity and duration, it's important to make sure that you give yourself ample time to rest and recuperate before continuing on with your trip. Additionally, if you do come down with a bout of food poisoning it's important to keep yourself well hydrated by drinking plenty of fluids, especially those containing electrolytes such as Powerade or Gatorade and maximising your rest by spending the time in bed. Additionally a visit to the pharmacist is a good idea as they will be able to provide medication to assist in alleviating your symptoms. If symptoms persist for more than 24 hours, or they increase in severity, it's best to visit a doctor or hospital to check that it's not something more serious.

Bed Bugs
While uncommon in the majority of reputable hostels bed bugs can be brought in from an outside source by other travellers after travelling in sleeping

bags, clothing or rucksacks. Often the first sign of bed bugs will be bites and scratching these will only inflame them even more. If you do find your bed contains bedbugs it's best to notify the hostel as soon as possible and try to arrange to move to a new bed or room to avoid the problem. If your hostel isn't 24 hours and there's a spare bed available change your sleeping attire and move to the new bed to try and minimise your chances of being bitten. Avoid placing your bag on beds in a hostel as well as leaving clothes on the bed, as this can result in the spread of bedbugs. Any clothing or sleeping equipment that has come into contact with bedbugs should be washed thoroughly in hot water and tumble dried for a half hour if the fabric permits you to do so as this will help to remove and kill the bedbugs left lingering.

Rabies and Tetanus

While it's definitely advised to get your rabies and tetanus shots before leaving on your trip for those of you who may have missed them it's important to know what to do when you may come into contact with these while travelling. If you're bitten by an animal such as a monkey or a dog it's advisable to scrub the bite under running water for five minutes and to soak the wound with diluted iodine or other disinfectant while doing so. Even if you've received your immunisation prior to travelling, a post-bite injection is required to ensure that you haven't contracted rabies. This should be done as soon as possible and at most no later than 72 hours from the time you were first bitten.

Sunburn

Often one of the most overlooked aspects when travelling, and one of the most common, is sunburn. While the best precautions to sunburn involve applying sunscreen and wearing both a shirt and hat even the most prudent traveller can end up sunburnt after spending a day walking around a city. Apply aloe vera or after-sun gel to the affected areas, drink plenty of fluids and avoid long periods in the sun until the burns have cleared up. If your skin has blistered and these begin to burst apply an antiseptic cream to prevent the possibility of infection and to assist the wound in healing.

Being considerate

What constitutes 'considerate' behaviour varies greatly from country to country, but there are a few universal rules you can abide by which will see you well receive no matter where you travel:

- Ask for permission: If you want to take a photograph of some children playing or a pair of old men playing checkers in a park it's polite to ask permission before doing so, in the same way that you would likely take offence if someone suddenly arrived and began pointing a camera in your face and taking photos without first asking permission.

- Respect the locals: If your guide or guidebook asks you not to take photographs of women, as is the case in Morocco, then be respectful and don't take photographs of women unless you've expressly received their consent to do so. These requests aren't made simply to stop you from taking some good photographs; rather they have to do with cultural, spiritual or social beliefs.

- Remove your shoes when entering someone's house. In the majority of countries around the world it's expected that you will remove your footwear when entering a house, and in a lot of cases you will be presented with a pair of 'house slippers' to wear instead.

- Don't use your left hand. It may seem unusual to avoid using your left hand when eating or shaking hands with someone until you realise that the left hand is used to clean up after going to the bathroom in a lot of places such as Asia.

- Go with the flow. If a family has invited you into their home to share a meal and they want to say a prayer beforehand now is not the time to begin a debate on what is the correct religion (if any) or to share your personal beliefs on prayer. Instead embrace the experience as a cultural event and use it as an opportunity to see how others live their life on a day to day basis.

Tipping and Donations

Tipping and donations can often be confusing, especially when travelling abroad for the first time. While the etiquette at home may be second nature to you, it can often be quite different abroad and a great example of contrasting tipping etiquette can be found between the United States and Japan. In the US tipping is commonplace, with the expectation that a tip of 15-25% should be left on top of your bill when eating out, as this tip makes up a large portion of your servers wages while in Japan leaving a tip is seen as insulting, as if you're taking pity on the server and feel they're a charity case.

While, of course, there's no such thing as a universal policy when it comes to tipping in any one country, if you're unsure of how much you should tip, or even if you should tip, the best thing to do it to leave a tip of 10%, unless you feel a need to tip otherwise. Outside of the United States and Japan, a 10% tip shows your appreciation without raising too much surprise from your server. Remember, if you're travelling to poorer countries, a tip of even one or two dollars can be the equivalent to a day's wages for some staff.

When it comes to donations, everybody has a different opinion on how you should best handle beggars, children and others who may ask you for money during your travels. While the humanitarian in you no doubt wants to help everyone, it's not uncommon to give money or food to one disadvantaged person and suddenly several more appear out of nowhere asking where their donation is.

In some instances, such as those made famous in *Slumdog Millionaire* children are actually injured or disfigured by gang members in order to attract more sympathy and any money given to these kids actually goes directly to the gang rather than the kids themselves. It's a brutal reality and not one that you want to inadvertently support by giving to beggars. It's best to avoid giving money at the time and instead support a locally based charity instead that focuses on providing much needed services such as food, water or education to people rather than giving them cash directly.

Insurance Claims

While the majority of travellers never need to lodge a travel insurance claim, it's important to know what to do in the event that something goes wrong. Firstly if you have the number of your insurance company handy give them a call as soon as conveniently possible to let them know that an incident has occurred that may result in you needing to lodge a claim. In the event of thefts, most companies will require a police statement containing the details of the theft which must be completed at a local police station, while medical expenses, such as doctors' visits or hospital trips, will require a bill to be presented as proof of expenses incurred.

In the event your flight is delayed or your luggage doesn't appear, you may find yourself covered, depending on your insurance policy and this will vary dramatically depending on your level of coverage. Nonetheless, it's always best to give your company a call to clarify what is covered if something happens as you can always claim these expenses back at the conclusion of your trip if you'd rather not deal with it mid travelling, provided you have let them know of the incident when it happens. Most policies will have clauses that exclude you from payout if you've been drinking, have a pre-existing related medical condition that you did not inform them of or if you're injured while participating in extreme sports such as white water rafting or snowboarding. Keep a copy of your policy's fine print sitting in your email inbox for reference if needed.

Contacting Home

Calling home

Calling friends and family has never been easier than it is now. Even ten years ago, calls were made using a prepaid phone card at a public payphone whereas now you can call home for free via the internet, provided you have a connection. Unless you're trekking well out of the way of cities and towns, there will be plenty of cafes, hostels, fast food places and coffee shops that offer Wi-Fi and a chance to call home. Alternately you can purchase a local prepaid sim card, load credit onto it and use this for making calls. Though more expensive, you have the added advantage of being able to make calls anywhere there is mobile reception rather than strictly internet as well as being able to make local calls as well, which may come in handy when organising things such as day trips. Additionally, ensure that global roaming is turned off on your phone, as calls made and received from your regular phone are charged at a much higher rate than you would pay at home.

Mail

While somewhat old fashioned and much slower than an email or a call sending home a postcard is a great way to stay in touch with friends and family back home. Alternately, send home a postcard to your future self, complete with everything you've done in the city or country; it makes a great souvenir later in life and it allows you to keep a collection of your favourite memories. Additionally, it may be cheaper to ship home gifts and presents, such as clothing, rather than paying extra for carry-on luggage on your return flight; just be aware that parcel delivery times and prices vary greatly depending on where you're sending your mail from and the dimensions and weight of the parcel.

Departure Tax and bribes

When departing countries always double check the day before if you're required to pay a departure tax or produce any documentation on departure. While some places such as most of the Balkans will not require this at all as this is built into the price of your ticket other countries, such as Australia, require a departure tax to be paid before leaving the country. Ensure that you have the correct amount available in cash to make the process as hassle-free as possible.

Occasionally this departure tax may not be official at all, rather it's a small bribe solicited by border guards to make your crossing hassle free and this is more likely to occur when crossing borders in second and third world countries, especially by land. In the event that you're required to give a 'payment' to cross the border never mention the word 'bribe' at all, as this is insinuating that it's an illegal activity. Instead, overlooking the fact that it quite clearly is a bribe; simply ask how much the payment is and who the payment should be made to. You will find that often higher payments can be negotiated down, especially if you're able to throw a couple of cigarettes or some alcohol into the deal as a sweetener. Be respectful and calm at all times, as yelling or accusations of corruption are going to get you blocked from entry in the best case scenario or arrested if you've already crossed over in the worst case scenario.

Printed in Great Britain
by Amazon